FAIRY TAIL

HIRO MASHIMA

12

12 CONTENTS

Chapter 92: Destiny — 3

Chapter 93: Pray to the Sacred Light — 23

Chapter 94: One Person — 43

Chapter 95: Sleeping Beauty Warrior — 63

Chapter 96: Meteor — 83

Chapter 97: A Life as a Shield — 103

Chapter 98: Dragon Force — 123

Chapter 99: Titania Falls — 143

Chapter 100: To Tomorrow! — 165

Translation Notes — 200

Chapter 92: Destiny

SHLIK

In fifteen minutes...

!!

L-Lost. That is...the first time...that has happened...since I entered the guild...

However, you will lose too... to Jellal...

Ah...

SLUMP

That poem was terrible...

Fall down upon us; O light of divine justice; Bring death to us all!

!

Quickly, gather up Simon and the others, along with my friends from the guild, and get as far away from here as you can!

Shô, you're wounded. Can you walk?

Y-Yeah... I think so...

Fifteen minutes?

Is she talking about Etherion?

9

You will do as I ask, won't you...

...Shô?

B-But...

What about you, sis?

TMP
ひた
ひた TMP

Yeah.

I'll meet you, but first...

...I'm going to end this!

!

Huh?

Wha—?!!

So you're awake, Natsu?

Stop that!!! Don't get sick just remembering!!!

URP!

UWOOO...

I was riding on this weird moving vehicle...

That cat flew him from the tower.

But Gray was pretty beaten up in the battle too.

After that, you were eaten by Fukuro and saved by Gray.

By Gray?!!

Hey! Focus!

I just know he's going to use this against me for a whole month!!! He's the kind of guy who never knows when a joke gets old! *DAMMIT!*

I don't know if I'd call it "losing." You were eaten.

Arrrgg!!! It isn't possible!!! How can I lose and Gray win?!!!

This isn't the time for stunts like that!!!!

GWIP

I can't let this stand!!!! I need revenge!!!! I'm going off to fight that dumb Fukuro again!!!!

This time, I'll do it with an arm tied behind my back!!!! If I have a handicap like that, then—

GURK!

I'm Simon. Erza's old friend.

By the way, who are you again?

SLUMP

D-Don't worry about me... Just listen, Natsu...

Hey, are you hurt?!

They didn't understand the situation, but with some persuasion, I got them to take your friends out of the tower.

Myaa! Simon says they're allies now!

Weren't these guys supposed to be enemies?

ZGGL ZGGL

A little while ago, I got a message from Wally and Millia.

They found Lucy, Juvia, and one of the Trinity Raven passed out in a hall.

She said she was going to finish all of this.

The only one left is Jellal, and Erza is going after him.

But I didn't beat any of them!!!

Soon after, I got a message from Shô saying that all three of the Trinity Raven have been defeated.

...but Jellal is much too powerful...

A fight to the death may be an unavoidable destiny for them...

Fate has bound those two for eight years.

!!?
•••

I don't wanna!

So please!!! Go rescue Erza!!!

Is it really so fun to play games with people's lives?

SST

Well, it looks like the game is almost over.

ROLL ROLL

KALUNK

Or to put it another way, life on its own is boring and empty.

Within the balance of life and death is the origin and sum of all emotions.

"Fun?" Yes, it is.

It's been a while...

...Erza.

Jellal.

You could have escaped whenever you felt like it, you know.

Take them. I don't need them anymore.

The Tower of Heaven is complete!

I'm here to free my former friends.

FSSH

No... Etherion will fall.

You're too relaxed. It was a trick after all, wasn't it?

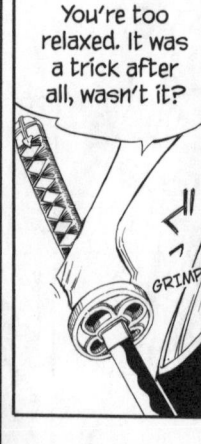

GRIMP

You mean Etherion?

HEH HEH...

Even if it will be destroyed in ten minutes?

You... refuse to save your friend...?

Refuse to rescue Erza?!!

This isn't a problem I can go sticking my nose in.

He's Erza's enemy. Erza can finish him off herself.

Who do you think Erza is, you jerk?!!!!

Erza can never beat Jellal!!!!

Chapter 93: Pray to the Sacred Light

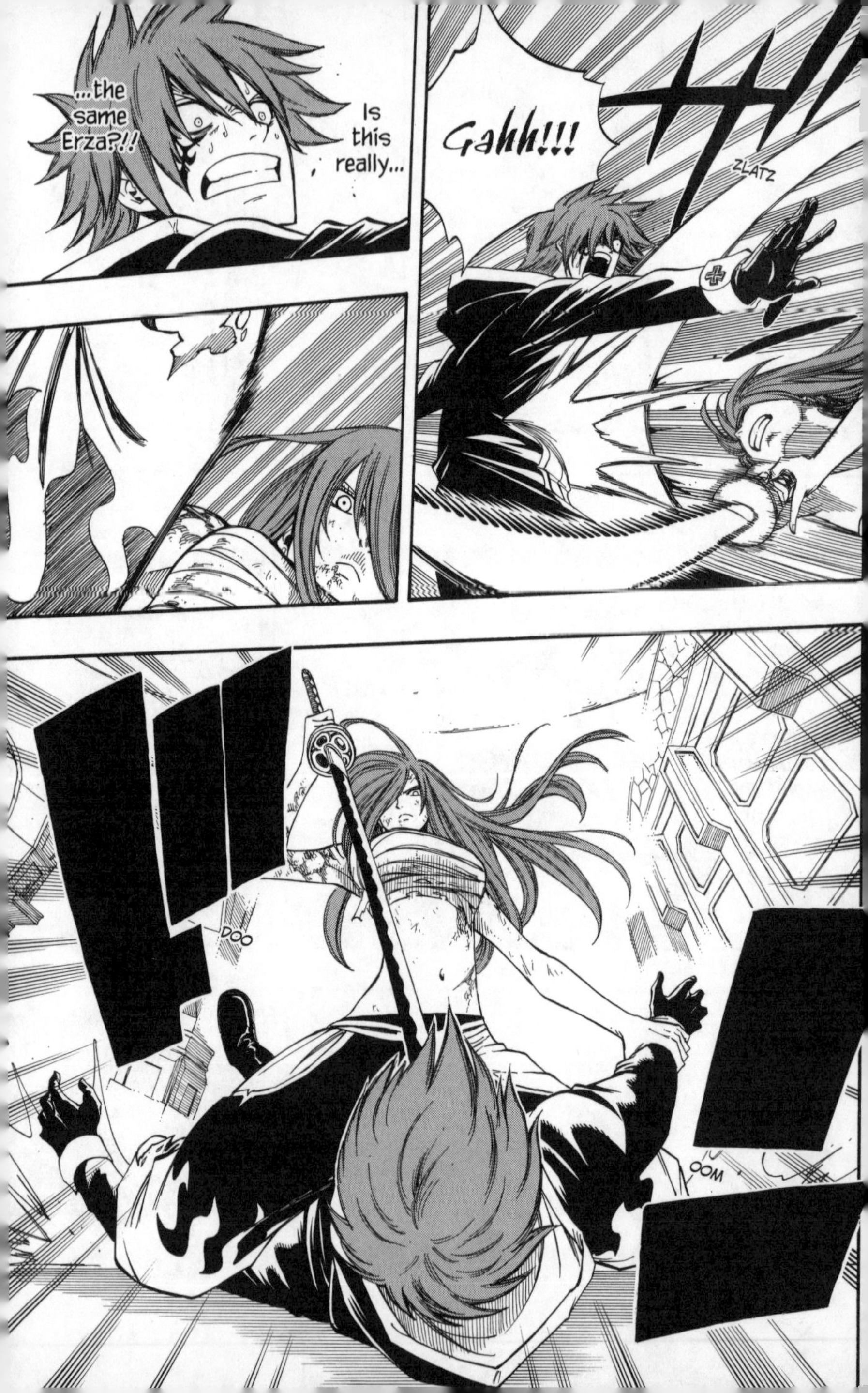
Is this really...
...the same Erza?!!
Gahh!!!
ZLATZ
DOO
OOM

So what is your real purpose behind all this?

Kh!

It's true the principles and construction would be exactly as it was in the plans...

...but there was one very important element missing.

You didn't think I'd spend eight years doing nothing, did you?

I did my research on the R-System.

You really haven't finished the R-System, have you?

!!!

What's missing is...

...the magic power!!!

I'm talking about even before the sacrifice!

I already told you about that... The sacrifice was you.

To power such an enormous magical device...

You could gather every wizard on the continent, and still not be sure you'd have power on that scale.

...you will need more than 270 million edea of magic power!!

......

Not only could one person not do it, but this tower doesn't even have the capacity to store up that much power.

On top of that, you know about the Council's attack, and still you're not trying to escape.

That means you're plotting something!!!

So is it your desire to die here and now?!!!

Jellal!!! Your dream ended a long time ago!!!!

Three minutes until Etherion...

I'm going to hold you down here with my own hands until the final moment!!!!

If that's it, then we're both going together!!!!

Um...

Kh...

@SSH

That isn't such a bad idea...

A- All right...

I'm just a puppet he uses until he can revive his own flesh.

Zeref's spirit took over my body...

And he doesn't listen to me...

I couldn't save myself...

I couldn't save any of my friends...

"Took over?"

All of existence was finished before it ever even started.

There is no heaven.

Look where you want, you'll never find freedom either.

The final phase of the Etherion launch is complete!

Deploy the Satellite Square!!!

Our prayers go with it.

Our prayers go with it.

Our prayers go with it.

Our prayers go with it.

GM GM GM GM GM

Natsu... Erza...

Hurry up and get out of there...

Wait a second! Was the Council serious about sending down Etherion?!!

Myaa!

There's no way I could have been able to finish the R-System...

GM GM GM GM GM

...but Zeref's spirit wouldn't allow me to let up.

Erza...

I'm just a broken engine that he's driving.

No one...is able to stop him now.

That's why you came here, isn't it?

You win.

Kill me.

FWOOOOON

It's all over.

For you...

...and for me too.

KLAKK

SST

I don't have to do anything. You hear that screech, right?

The Satellite Square has been deployed, targeting this tower.

So you're just another of Zeref's victims?

You always were a clumsy person, huh?

There was such a huge divide between my dream and reality, my heart couldn't face it.

It's my own fault. I was defeated by my weakness.

Erza...

...are the ones you call your friends.

The only ones who can save you from your own weaknesses and insufficiencies...

I have...

Now, I'll pay for the crime of not being able to save you.

...been saved.

Chapter 94: One Person

Etherion...

Was the attack a success?!! Get me confir- mation fast!!!

I repeat, direct hit by Etherion !!!

Direct hit by Etherion !!!

Era...

We predict extreme weather conditions!

The density of Ethernano fusion is increasing!

It's impossible to avoid a few sacrifices when we need to stop that.

They were organized with the purpose of reviving Zeref.

I wonder how many people were in that tower.

...that won't alleviate the loss of the families of those sacrificed.

What-ever our justifi-cations...

Natsu...

Erza...

The outer walls have all crumbled away...

...and the interior was... crystal?

Wh-What...

...is that...?

Natsu and Erza...and that guy Simon...?

Say... They're okay, right?

What happened to this place... and what's it changed into?

Oww...

Etherion fell...

Wh-Why am I still...

Finally the time has come!!!!

Finally!!!!

Does this surprise you, Erza?

Heh heh heh...

You...

And because of the Council and Etherion...

This is the true form of the Tower of Heaven!!

It is a giant lacrima crystal!!

You were so cute, Erza!

S-So that was all a trick, huh...?

What ?!

Wh-What are you doing here?!!

Still... since we have exactly the same face, it's only natural.

You mistook me for Jellal and attacked.

I remember the first time we met, Erza.

You came to turn in case reports to the Council with Makarov.

But your hostility never abated.

HYUUOOOOOOO

You finally were talked down when I told you we were twins.

At the time I should have said something that would have convinced you that I was going to find Jellal and kill him.

Ah, yes. That was a mistake of mine.

Even worse... you were spying on me for him!!!

What did you expect?!! You spent all your time covering up what Jellal was doing rather than stopping him as a brother should!!!

So you two...were in collusion all along, huh?

There's nothing more painful than those excuses made up on the spot, is there?

But my biggest mistake was to encounter you at all, right after becoming a member of the Council.

"Collusion"? That isn't quite the right word.

He vanished...

Sieg... just disappeared!

Exactly
!

Sieg
is me.

Thought
projec-
tion?!!!

I-If that's the case, then you dropped Etherion down on your own head!!!

Is that the whole reason you wormed your way onto the Council?!!

I don't believe it!!!

Of course that and everything else was all a part of Zeref's plan to be revived.

Was your transient freedom enjoyable, Erza?

FAIRY TAIL

Chapter 95:
Sleeping Beauty Warrior

That's the real form of the R-System that we helped to build.

It's started up!!

What?!!

It's the R-System!!!

I don't know... It's the first time that we've seen it started up too.

Started up, you say?!!

You don't mean they're reviving Zeref, do you?!!

67

Where is that might you showed a little while ago?

Did you use up all your magical power fighting with Ikaruga?

Unff!!

ZUSHAAA

WHOOSH

GM GM GM GM GM GM GM GM GM GM

ZLMM ZLMM ZLMM

Jellal..

GRIMP

Jellal!!!!

Really ?!

F-Forgive me... My body... can't move...

Natsu... You have to get out of here now...

HA HA HA HAAA!!!

S-Stop it...

TICKLE

TICKLE

TICKLE

TICKLE

You're always giving me beatings I can never forget!! Well take this!!!

You don't know who you're fighting...

You don't know enough about him to beat him!!!

I don't wanna! If you don't want to do it yourself, I'll do the fighting for you!

No...!

Please...

BLUP

Do what I say...

You're saying that if I don't know, I can't win?

GWIMM?

Yo!

Wh-What are you...

What?

Erza, I don't know enough about you either.

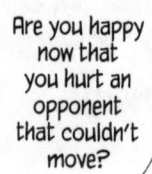

Are you happy now that you hurt an opponent that couldn't move?

......

You're even more outrageous than the rumors say.

...was crying.

Erza...

She's at her best when she's strong and violent!!!

I don't ever want to see Erza like that!!!

She spit out her words in that weak whisper, and her voice was quavering.

FAIRY TAIL

Name: Laki Olietta **Age:** 18 yrs.

Magic: Wood Make

Likes: Glasses **Dislikes:** Lechers

Chapter 96: Meteor

Remarks

A Wood Make wizard. She uses a magic that can take any wooden material and, in an instant, transform it into any shape she desires. Because of that talent, she has had very little sleep during the reconstruction of the guild.

She likes to use odd turns of phrase. Recently she cut her hair, but within her group of friends, she calls it "severing her hair." Other phrases include "feeding the stomach" for "eating" and "enduring the defenseless time" for "sleeping."

TMP

GWOOOOO

I'd hoped to have a taste of a dragon slayer's magic before I personally wiped them off the face of the Earth.

POFF はあん

POFF はあん

What was that? !!!

EDMP

If that's all you can do, then you lack the substance to back up the awe you inspire.

For that, I think I'll turn you into fodder for my *heavenly body* magic.

But you did interfere with my ritual.

CHASSH

WHUD

It's amazing your body is still in one piece.

This kind of destruction magic is like being hit by a falling meteor.

Its magical power is already starting to leak out.

It wouldn't be good for the R-System to take any more damage.

But I must say that I may have overdone it a bit.

Mustn't we, Erza?

We must hurry.

!

TONK

TONK

KLAK.

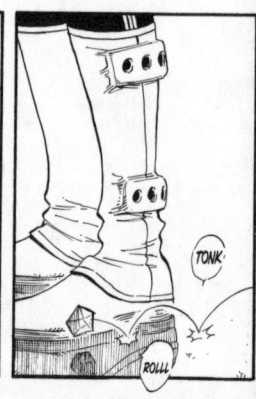

TONK

ROLL

HAHH HAHH
HAHH HAHH
KRIK
HUP
TONK
TONK
......
ガリ
SHF
TONK
コォ
HYUUUM
TONK
TONK
HUP
ヨT

Heh heh...

...my attack...

...hit you...

THUNK

Then this is not your lucky day!!!!

Don't do that!!!!

GOO

OOM

This tower... This crystal? You just said damage wouldn't be good for it, right...?

GRRNN

...of everybody in Fairy Tail.

Breaking things is a specialty...

Well, I'm fired up now!!!

More than I've ever been before!!!!

You little punk...

FAIRY TAIL

Chapter 97:
A Life as a Shield

I'm going to finish you in an instant!!

You'll regret standing up to me when you're on your way to hell!!!

So if you can take me down, go ahead and try!!!

One thing I know about me is that I can take punishment.

!!!

DOGOOOOM

...Kôen
!!!!*

*Fire Dragon's Gleaming Flame.

He's...
targeting
the
tower...

SKRRRRRCH

WHOOSH

!!!

Do you dare kill me?!!!

Zeref needs a sacrifice to be revived, right?!!

But now that it's come to this, it doesn't have to be you!!!

Yes...One condition is that the body be of a wizard that is fit to be a wizard saint.

Erza!!! Get out of the way!!!

Bow to your death!!!

Both of you together...

!!

You have nothing to worry about!!!

I will protect you!!!

heavenly body magic...

...Altairis!!!!

No!!! Don't!!!!

DOO

OOM

SLUMP

Er...

...za...

Simon...

Was that bug still crawling around this place?

THUD

Simon!!!

Why didn't you...

..escape like the others?!!

I knew... that someday...

KAFF!

...I could...

...help... you...

OFF...

I-I'm... glad...

HAHH

HAHH

Simon !!!

HAHH HAHH

You... were... always so... sweet...

...so kind...

HAHH HAHH

Okay, I under-stand!!! Now don't try to speak anymore!!

I've always...

Simon...

...

...loved you...

HAHH HAHH

!!

THUNK

AH HA HA HA HA HA

How pitiful!!!

The most pitiful thing I've ever seen!!!!

Simon!!!!

TWITCH

They call that "dying in vain," don't they!!?

This changes absolutely nothing!!! No matter what you do, nobody is leaving this tower alive!!!

Nooooooo!!!!!

FAIRY TAIL

Chapter 98:
Dragon Force

...eating Etherion?!!

He is...

GAH-HAHH!!!

What are you doing this for?!! It's stupid!!!

Ethernanos are fused with all sorts of power, not just flame!!!

GURK

GURK

What?! Does he think he can power up with any magical power, even if it isn't fire?

GAHH!!

GWAHHH!!!

Natsu!!!

AAAAAAA

AAAAA

With messed-up logic like that, he'll finish himself off for me!!

What?!!

A dragon?!!

GUU

GOO

OOMM

Im-

Impos-
sible!!!

It's my
destiny
to create
a land of
freedom
!!!!

I
can't be
defeated
!!!

That's right... I'm the only one who can feel Zeref!!!

In my fear and pain, Zeref whispered to me!!!

He quietly asked me if I wanted true freedom!!!

KANG

KANG

KANG

KANG

Together with Zeref, I will create a nation of true freedom!!!!

I am the chosen one!!!!

And you tried to make it by stealing the freedom of everybody else!!!!

Why don't you stupid people understand that?!!!

Only the will to change the world can alter history!!!

All I need is another eight years... No, I can complete it in five...

Is he going to destroy everything, including the tower?!!!

Zeref... just you wait!!!

Is that an Abyss Break?!!!

Kh...

ZLATZ

!!! ZHAAN

!!

You won't ever get your freedom!!!!

DMM

No jerk whose will is controlled by ghosts can ever find freedom!!!!

CHASSH

GWOOM

DOO

OOM

Is this Natsu's true power....?

Chapter 99:
Titania Falls

He defeated as powerful a man as Jellal...

My fight, a fight that's been going on for eight years, is over.

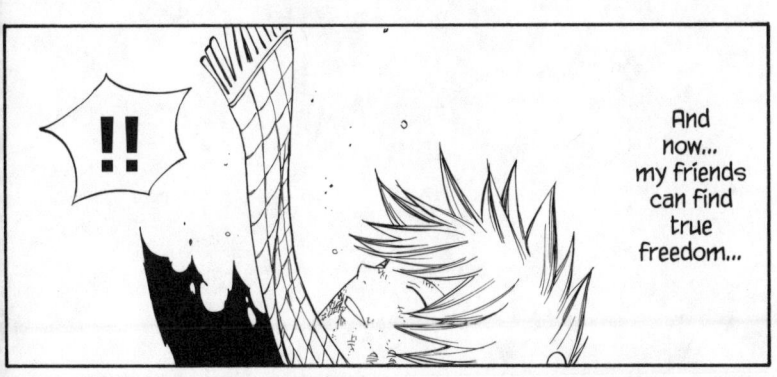

!!

And now... my friends can find true freedom...

Natsu!!!

DMP

SLUMP

GRI

IMP

!

You really are amazing.

Truly!

パ
PCHUU
ヒュ
ィ

バ
BWAAA
オ
オ

BAM
バ
ッ

I-It couldn't be that Etherion is out of control, could it?!!

What is that?!!

The tower...!!!

GM コ
GM
GM コ
GM コ
GM

Basically anything trying to contain that much magical power in one place would be unstable...

Out of control ?!!

What about sis and the others inside?!!

Wait a second!! With us this close, we're going to—

It's bursting out and causing an explosion...

It's a tidal wave of magical power with no place to go...

We're in danger here...

There's something more urgent than who can be rescued and who can't...

...of complete destruc-tion!!!

GWOO

DOOM

GWAA OOM

CRUMBLE

ズシェェ…
ZUSHAAA

Umphh…

With things as they are, even if we get outside the building, we'll still be caught up in the blast!!!

It looks to have a lot more destructive power than I ever imagined!!!

This magic power is warping its container... the lacrima crystal...

Dammit !!!

Does it all end here?!!

No...

When did I ever give up?!!

SHKK

DMM

DMM

This time, it's my turn to rescue you...

...Natsu!!!

So what do I do...?!!

But it's impossible to contain the blast or even escape...

"Fuse"?

"And it will break down your body into its smallest components only to reform as Zeref's body."

"That 270 million edea of magical power stored in the lacrima will fuse with your body."

I'll just have to risk it!!!!

...then the power will use my body as its container and I can stop the explosion.

If I can fuse with the Etherion energy...

Good!!! The lacrima crystal is allowing my body inside!!!

Errnn...

ZUPUMM

Arrg!!!

Natsu?!!

Erza...

This is the only way to stop Etherion.

Your... body is going into the—

What... are you doing...?

GOCHAAA

GWOO

Stop Etherion...?

Don't be stupid!!! If you do that, you'll—!!!

But if I can fuse with Etherion, I may be able to absorb the energy...

Pretty soon, Etherion will go out of control and destroy the tower in a huge explosion.

ZLMM

ZLMM

ZLMM

Uwaah !!!

ZLMM

ZLMM

Stop it!!! Erza!!!

Aaa ah !!!

ZLMM
ZLMM
ZLMM

SKRRCH

GMP.

Erza!!!

Natsu...

Don't do it!!!

Don't worry! I'll figure out a way to stop it...

I can't even imagine life without my friends.

If it weren't for Fairy Tail, I wouldn't have been able to go on.

To me, you guys are...

...as important as the whole world.

Erza...

...I'd trade this body...

...then without a moment's hesitation...

If it's possible for me to save you...

...to see you live!!!!

ZLZT

!!!

IIMM

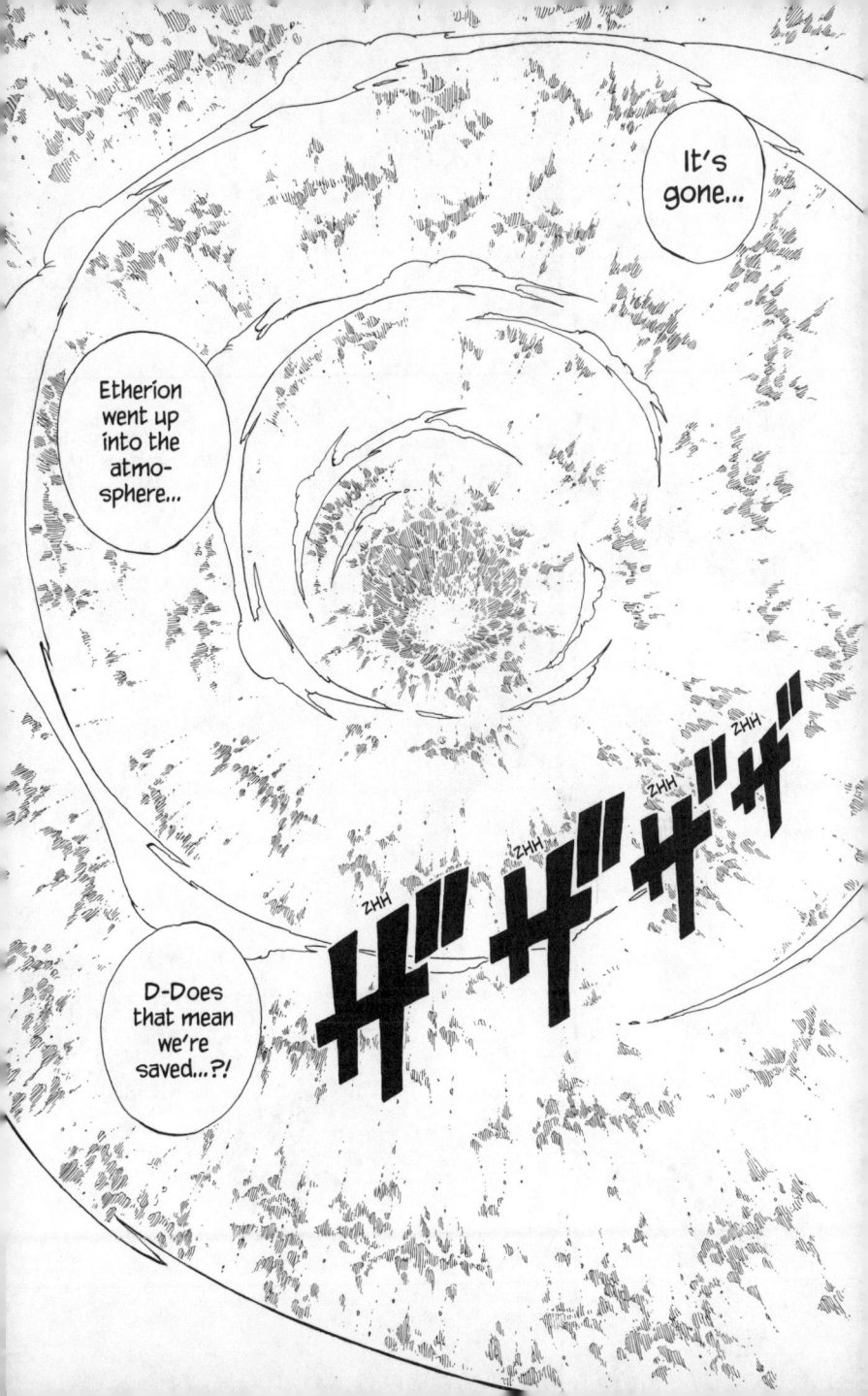

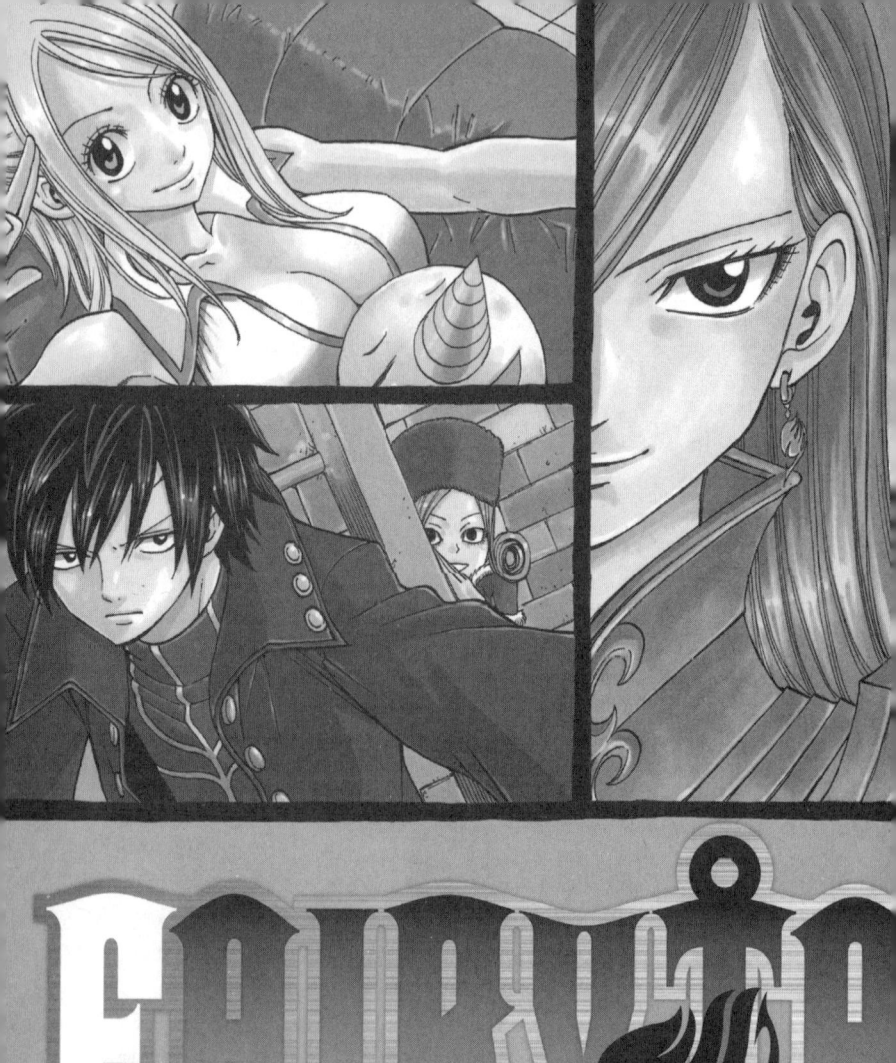

Chapter 100: To Tomorrow!

······

ぱさ本
FSHHH

Well?

I-It's fixed...

Can you see through it?

Yes.

Where am I?!!

No, that isn't it... This place is far more warm...

Inside Etherion?!

Oh!

!

HI' HI'

SHHHHHH

Erza Scarlet
Rest in peace

Am...

Am I
dead?

This woman... Erza Scarlet...

SHHHH HI'' HI'' HI'' HI''

SHHHHH

HI'' HI'' HI''

SHHHH

And she loved us, her friends, as well.

...was loved by the gods, and she loved them.

HI''

SHH

She moved in the way fairies dance, and she was lovelier than the finest scene nature can produce.

Her heart was as big and limitless as the sky.

Her sword glistened nobly, and was used only for those she loved.

ERZA SCARLET

It is love that makes one strong!

But what makes one weak is also love.

And I...

SNIFF

SNIFF

SNIFF...

...I loved her as a true member of my family...

SNIFF SNIFF

SNIFF SNIFF SNIFF

Master...

SHHHHHH

...for the peaceful repose of her soul...

I pray...

SHHHH

SHKK

SHKK

SHKK

SHKK

The Council, in a unanimous decision, with a single empty seat...

...have taken up a resolution to honor this woman.

SHKK

SHKK

FASSH

These are a waste!!!

Natsu...

Stop that now, Natsu!!!!

Erza isn't dead!!!

You jerk!!

Natsu, don't...

Wake up to reality, for pity's sake!!!!

She can't be dead, right?!!!

Please, Natsu... Don't!

Erza's still alive !!!!

Let go of me !!!!

CLAMOR

CLAMOR

CLAMOR

But...

GAN

NCH

I did it... for Natsu's future...

Is this the future of everyone left behind?

Is this their future?

I just did it so that everybody could smile again...

I didn't want to see a future like this!!

I'm begging you... Please stop crying like that...

I can't...

Make it stop!

I can't do this...

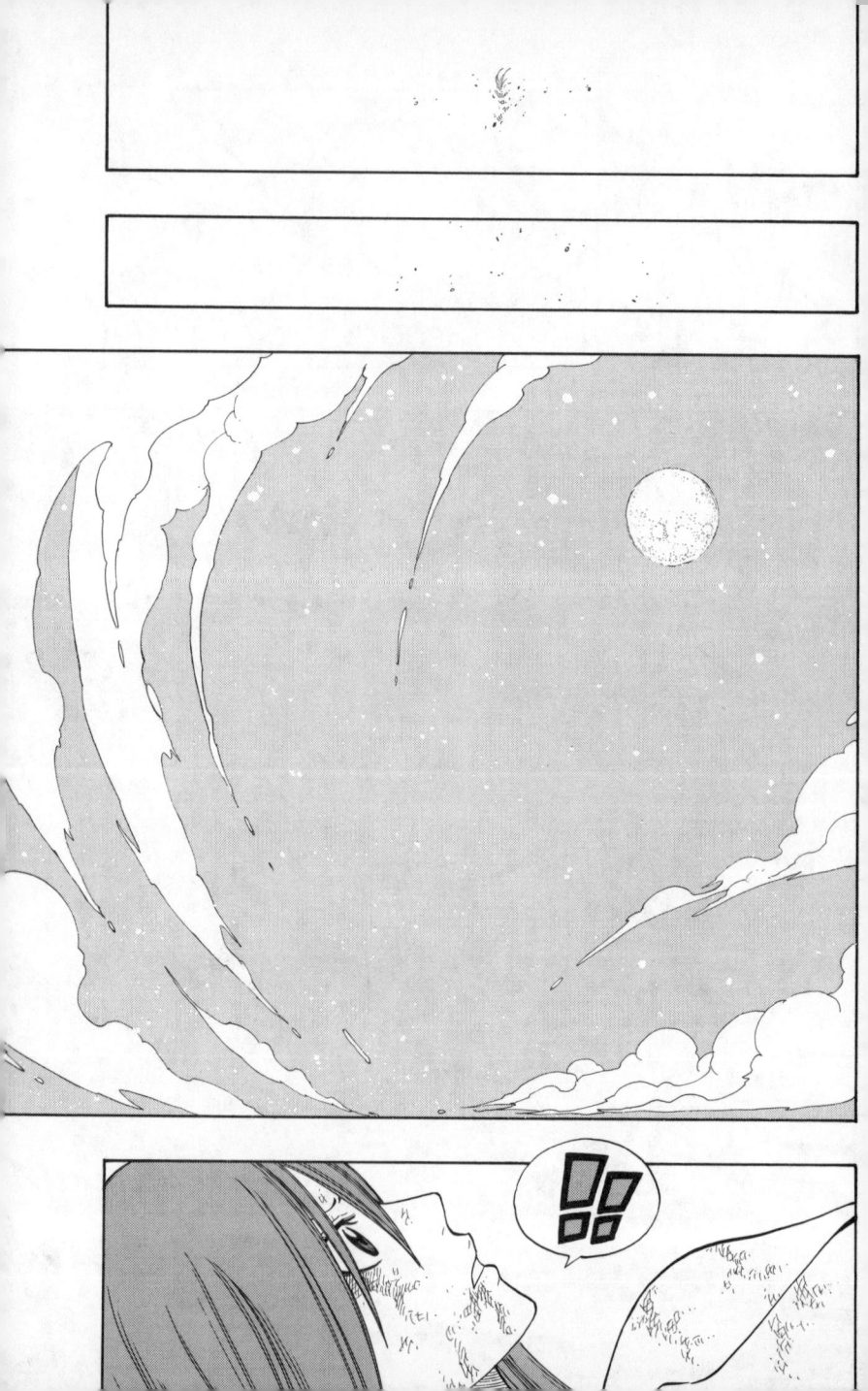

SPASH SPASH SPASH

!

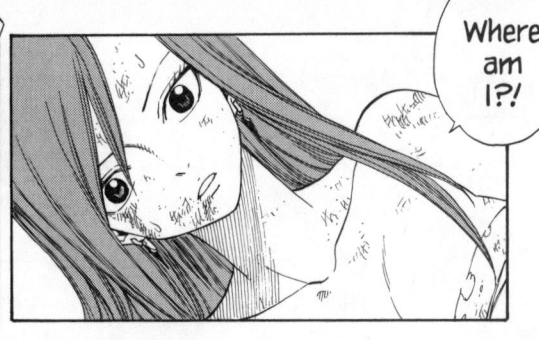

Where am I?!

Erza !!!!

SPASH

SPASH

SPASH

SPASH

SPASH

It's so wonderful that you're all right!!!!

What did you have to go worrying us like that for?!!

What... happened here?

Sis !!!!

Am I...

...alive?

But... how...?

Natsu...

You saved me?

Could he have found me inside that huge tornado of magic power...?

Wh-What kind of man can do that...?

It's the same for me.

What?

SLUMP

SPAA

AASH

It's the same for all of us...

"If it weren't for Fairy Tail, I wouldn't have been able to go on."

"I can't even imagine life without my friends."

Don't ever do that again...

Never again !!!!

Natsu...

HIK...

SNIFF SNIFF

Because that is the path that leads to a happy future...

TO BE CONTINUED

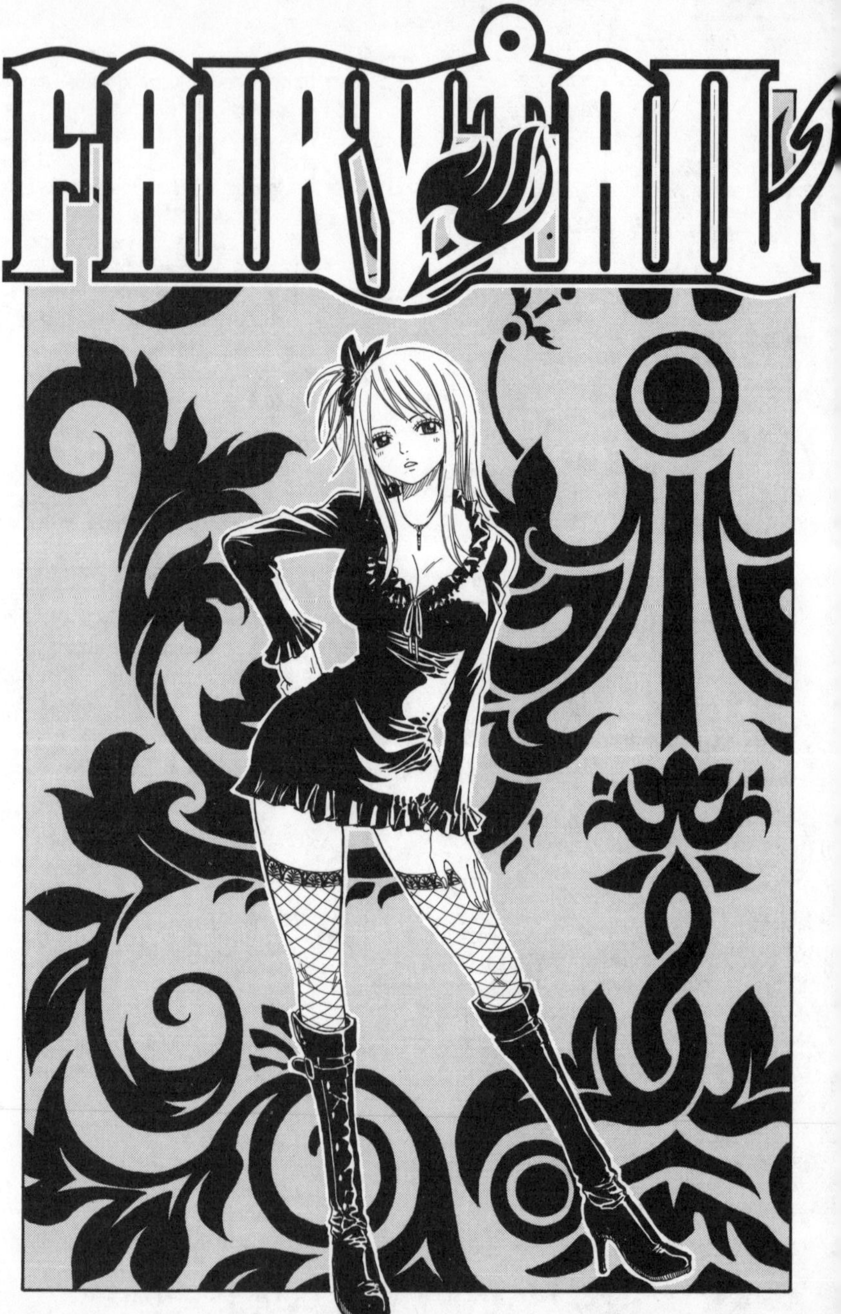
FAIRY TAIL

Mira: Next question!

*If Shô was
stuck in the
tower all that
time, why is he
so suntanned?*

 : There it is!! The question that points out problems with the whole setup!!

 : The answer must be that he wasn't inside the tower for that entire time.

Lucy: You...think so?

Mira: He made it all the way to the hotel on Akane Beach, right? He must have had a little bit of freedom.

Lucy: I got it!! Shô-kun was the only one allowed to work on the tower's walls!! That's why he's so tanned!

 : All right!! We've solved it!!

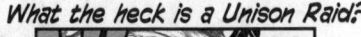 : "Solved it?" I just made a wild guess and threw it out for consideration...

Mira: With that, we come to the final question!

What the heck is a Unison Raid?

Lucy: I don't really know myself. It just happened by coincidence at the time...If we were asked to do it again, I don't think we could.

Mira: A Unison Raid is what it sounds like. It's an attack where two different types of magic become one, raising the attack level to one much higher than it would be if both were cast at the same enemy separately.

Lucy: Wooow!! I did something really incredible, didn't I?

 : They say that for all the recorded Unison Raids up to now, it could only happen between two friends so close they could almost read each other's thoughts. And even then, it's difficult.

Lucy: "Friends"...huh? Well, we can't claim that, but at the time...I'm sure that we really accepted each other on a very deep level, huh?

 : No, it was simply coincidence! Stomp, stomp, stomp....

 : ....

 : After you went and said something that sounded cool.

Lucy: ....

Mira: Oh, dear! What is the matter? Lucy's frozen up like a statue!

Lucy: ....

 : Okay, everybody! See you in the next volume!! Moun•tain•li•on•ponnn!!!

 : Hey!! That's my line!!!

Emergency Request
Explain the Mysteries of...
FAIRY TAIL?

From the Counter at Fairy Tail...

 : Moun•tain•li•on•ponnn!!!

 : What's that supposed to be?

Lucy: I thought the phrase would catch on. You know, something to get the people energized!
Moun•tain•li•on•ponnn!!!

Mira: You know, I really doubt it's going to catch on.

Lucy: You're probably right.

Mira: And...straight to the first question.

That scar on Natsu's neck... What's it from?

Lucy: We get this question a lot!

Mira: That's true...I think it's the most common question.

Lucy: But I've got to say that I'm amazed at how observant some people are!

Mira: What amazes me is with all those letters, we're only getting around to it now...

 : It's probably because the author hasn't thought up the answer yet, right?

 : That certainly is one possibility...

Lucy: Huh? What? You're saying there's some big secret behind it?

Mira: Anyway, the editor put in a word of advice on this, and taking that advice to heart, this matter is a s•e•c•r•e•t! ♡

 : I get the feeling that we didn't do anything to answer the question...

Lucy: So, on to the next question.

Those suits of Erza's armor that were cut to pieces, are they gone forever? I really loved the fire empress armor...

Lucy: The fire empress armor. It certainly is popular, isn't it?

Mira: Of course! It's Erza in twin ponytails!

Lucy: And the extremely high leg lines.

Mira: If she sends it out for repairs, she can get it fixed, right?

Lucy: Is *that* your answer?!!

Continued on the right-hand page.

TAIL d'ART

The *Fairy Tail* Guild d'Art is an explosion of fan art! Please send in your black-and-white art!! Those chosen to be published will get a signed mini poster! ♪ Make sure you write your real name and address on the back of your postcard!

▲ You realize that Ikaruga is the name of a bird, right? Fukuro (Owl) and Taka (Hawk) are just as their names say.

Kumamoto Prefecture, Hideyo Noguchi

◀ Whoa! Was Elfman ever looking this cool?!

Gunma Prefecture, STM

▲ This is a really great smile on Natsu! Just between you and me, Natsu's eyes are a little more catlike than most of the other characters.

Kagoshima Prefecture, Mai Nishimura

▲ Uwa ha ha ha ha!! This is incredibly good!! What makes it so cute?!!

Happy! Love it!! ♡

Fukushima Prefecture, Erumo

◀ Oohh!! If I ever actually come across a scene like this, I may be forced to do whatever the person wants!

Tôyama Prefecture, Tomoyo

◀ Huh? It looks like everybody's paired off into couples...

Saitama Prefecture, Maccha

● By sending in letters or postcards you give us permission to give your name, address, postal code and any other information you include to the author as is. Please keep that in mind.

▲ Uhyooh!! Everybody's in high-school uniforms!! This kind of picture could be turned into a key holder!

Saitama Prefecture, Leona

Send to: Hiro Mashima, Kodansha Comics
451 Park Ave. South, 7th Floor, New York, NY 10016

▲ Art from a Mirajane rocket!! You can see her in every Question Corner.

Gifu Prefecture, Yuki Mori

LEO OF THE LION PALACE

▲ Loke!! He hasn't had much of a part lately, but he'll show up again!! Watch for him! Fans!

Gifu Prefecture, Yuki

▲ Extremely well done!! It's like Lucy's face has a wonderful individuality to it!

FAIRY TAIL MASHIMA-SENSEI I HAD A BIG FAN OF YEARS AND I STARTED FICKING THIS WORKS UP RIGHT AFTER READING IT. IT'S LOADS OF FUN, AND I BUY EACH NEW VOLUME AS THEY COME OUT! I WANT TO SAY THAT I'M HOOKED! HERE IS A DRAWING OF LUCY AND HAPPY. I LOVE ALL THE QUIRKY CHARACTERS! IT'S FUN TO STAY! THESE TWO AS A PAIR! KEEP UP THE GREAT WORK!!

LUCY

Yamaguchi Prefecture,, I♡59

▲ Everybody pose for the picture!!! You really went for it! Thanks for drawing all of those characters!

Iwate Prefecture, Saaya

▲ A little Mirajane-chan! This kind of image is pretty rare!

Shizuoka Prefecture, Okara•Y

Re-jec-tion Cor-ner

Gifu Prefecture, Shōgo Hatanaka

D-Did this scene really have that much impact on the readers? Or was this all sent by people in the same family?

IT'S OLD-MAN CRUX'S TIME

NOW!!!

Yamaguchi Prefecture, Kiki Nakagawa

Hokkaido, Zeek

DYAAAAHA!!!!!

MASHIMA-SENSEI... KEEP AT IT!! I'VE BEEN A BIG FAN SINCE YOUR LAST SERIES!!

BURY ME IN THE REJECTED WORKS!!

Rejection

About the Creator

HIRO MASHIMA was born May 3, 1977, in Nagano Prefecture. His series *Rave Master* has made him one of the most popular manga artists in America. *Fairy Tail*, currently being serialized in *Weekly Shōnen Magazine*, is his latest creation.

AFTERWORD

The Erza chapter is over! Thank you for hanging in there!!! No, really, that's how I feel. I hung in, and I'm a little tired. But those last images in the book where Natsu and Erza are hugging—I really wanted to draw that!! I wanted to draw the scene where Erza was crying out of both eyes!! I worked hard through the whole story arc just to get to those. The fact that Erza could only cry out of one eye was something I had decided on at the beginning, and if you look at all the images of her crying, you'll see it foreshadowed in those...But there's one scene where I made a mistake and had tears streaming out of both eyes. (Sweat, sweat.) And I had paid so much attention to foreshadowing this fact too...so why?!! (Did I simply forget?)

Actually, this entire Erza chapter was a parody of my last work, *Rave Master*'s Etherion Chapter. Etherion. Sieg. Sieg's magic. The scene where Natsu is pictured on a black background and his taunts. The fireworks in the next volume too. All that and more were self parodies. Of course, if you don't know about it, it doesn't affect your enjoyment. But I hope those who do know get a small smile on their faces while reading it.

And while concentrating on other things like the above stuff, *Fairy Tail* has reached its one hundredth installment!!! Yaay! I never intended it to go on this long!!! I had thought that I'd stop this series at about ten volumes!! That's what I figured!!! But everybody's warm support got me all fired up!!! Or, to tell you the truth, I just don't think I've drawn enough of the story to finish it off. (Eh-heh!) While I'm in the middle of drawing *Fairy Tail*, I just keep coming up with new things that I want to draw. Even though I haven't even thought through to the next plot twist! (Ha ha.) And so, I'd like to thank you all for your support. I plan to try even harder in the future! In the next volume, we have a character show up again from the old days...(You mean that character's going to be a regular?!!)

Translation Notes

Japanese is a tricky language for most Westerners, and translation is often more art than science. For your edification and reading pleasure, here are notes on some of the places where we could have gone in a different direction in our translation of the work, or where a Japanese cultural reference is used.

Names

Hiro Mashima has graciously agreed to provide official English spellings for just about all of the characters in *Fairy Tail*. Because this version of *Fairy Tail* is the first publication of most of these spellings, there will inevitably be differences between these spellings and some of the fan interpretations that may have spread throughout the Web or in other fan circles. Rest assured that what is contained in this book are the spellings that Mashima-sensei wanted for *Fairy Tail*.

General Notes:
Wizard

In the original Japanese version of *Fairy Tail*, there are occasional images where the word "wizard" is found. This translation has taken that as its inspiration, and translated the word *madôshi* as "wizard". But *madôshi's* meaning is similar to certain Japanese words that have been borrowed into the English language, such as judo (the soft way) and kendo (the way of the sword). *Madô* is the way of magic, and *madôshi* are those who follow the way of magic. So although the word "wizard" is used, the Japanese would think less of traditional Western wizards, such as Merlin or Gandalf, and more of martial artists.

San Diego Comic-Con, page 202

The San Diego Comic-Con is America's largest comic-book convention, with an annual attendance of more than 120,000 in the past several years (including 2008, when Mashima-sensei went). Although it was traditionally a convention for American comic books, it has supported anime and manga since the 1980s, and has been a playground for such notable manga luminaries as Monkey Punch (*Lupin III*), Kia Asamiya (*Silent Möbius*), and Rumiko Takahashi (*Inu Yasha*) among many others. In the '90s and especially the decade of the 2000s, movie studios began to see the potential for viral marketing and started to play their previews and host Hollywood stars, directors, and crews in panels plugging their movies. There is even a panel for translators and editors of manga and anime, for any who want to know more about how their favorite manga is brought to English-speaking countries.

Ikaruga's poem, page 9

Ikaruga's poem is a haiku. Haiku is the most popular form of Japanese poetry. A standard haiku verse is a series of seventeen syllables separated into lines of five syllables, then seven, then five. See more about haiku in the notes for volume 11.

Grand Chariot, page 97

The seven stars Jellal is referring to form the constellation (star cluster) known to most American astronomers and astronomy hobbyists as the Pleiades. However, it is known in French as the Grand Chariot, and although the kanji in Jellal's dialog was written as "Seven Star Sword," the *furigana* pronunciation guide to the kanji reads, "Grand Chariot."

Shaved Ice, page 123

This image depicts a pretty standard summer scene in Japan. Shaved ice is one of the most popular summertime treats for children (and adults) in Japan. It is something like the popular treat, snowcones, in the West, but the amount of toppings is far more varied. Aside from the syrups found in snowcones, shaved ice can also be topped with such things as condensed milk, sweet beans, or matcha green tea.

Moun·tain·li·on·pooon! page 195

What she said in the Japanese was, "Ya·ma·ne·ko·pooon!" which basically means "Mountain Lion-pooon" with the "pooon" part being a meaningless sound intended to make the phrase a little cuter.

I went to a signing in San Diego, USA! Uwooh!! I was a little worried. What would I do if I went to the signing and nobody showed up? But my fears were groundless—a huge group of people were there, and the signing was a smashing success!! (Phew! That was a relief!) This is a picture of me going on a rampage when some nice fan gave me a scarf just like Natsu's!

—Hiro Mashima

Preview of Volume 13

We're pleased to present you with a preview from volume 13, now available from Kodansha Comics. Check out our Web site (www.kodanshacomics.com) for more details!

This time, he was lucky.

But such luck is not meant to last.

Like someone else I could mention?

HEH HEH

. . . . .

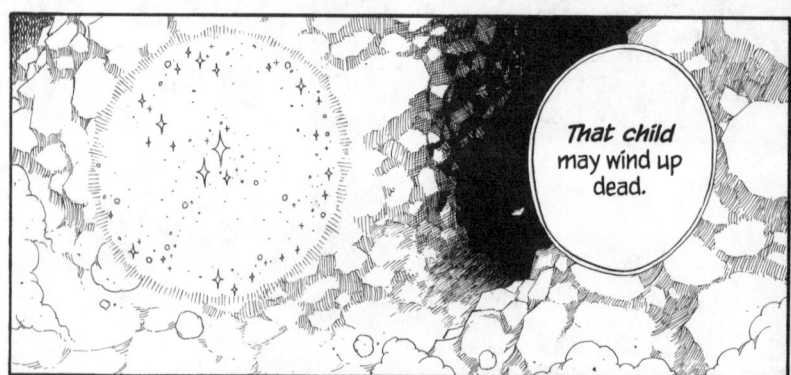

That child may wind up dead.

Leave !!!!

And do not interfere with the humans !!!!

I feel that eventually *that child* will meet up with Wendy.

This time, I hope they become good friends!

Leave!

Fairy Tail volume 12 is a work of fiction. Names, characters, places, and incidents are the products of the author's imagination or are used fictitiously. Any resemblance to actual events, locales, or persons, living or dead, is entirely coincidental.

A Kodansha Comics trade Paperback Original

Fairy Tail volume 12 copyright © 2008 Hiro Mashima
English translation copyright © 2010 Hiro Mashima

All rights reserved.

Published in the United States by Kodansha Comics, an imprint of Kodansha USA Publishing, LLC., New York.

Publication rights for this English edition arranged through Kodansha Ltd., Tokyo.

First published in Japan in 2008 by Kodansha Ltd., Tokyo

ISBN 978-1-612-62283-5

Printed in the United States of America

www.kodanshacomics.com

9

Translator/Adapter: William Flanagan
Lettering: North Market Street Graphics

D0204904